THE FLOOD, THE RE-BIRTH AND THE RACE

THE 21 SECRETS TO GET YOUR COMPANY'S REPUTATION TO THE TOP OF THE MARKET

THE FLOOD, THE RE-BIRTH AND THE RACE

THE 21 SECRETS TO GET YOUR COMPANY'S REPUTATION TO THE TOP OF THE MARKET

Noel Cardona

2018

First Printing: 2018

ISBN: 978-0-244-66190-8 (Paper Back)

www.Noelcardona.com

To Giovanna, my soulmate and the engine behind all my endeavors.

TABLE OF CONTENTS

ABOUT THE AUTHOR

First of all, let me thank you for picking up this book and hopefully, reading it. The majority of people will just pick a science fiction novel to read in their spare time with no intentions of growth. Don't get me wrong, we all need to rest but there needs to be time allocated to personal development.

I assume you are within the few who understand we are all limited by our own education. I encourage you to read this book in full, and most importantly, apply the concepts. If you have any questions you can find me at info@noelcardona.com. Also please join our community at www.noelcardona.com/21secrets to stay connected and share with other professionals who have common interests.

My name is Noel Cardona (Actually my full name is Noel Hernan Cardona Montoya) but let's keep it short. I am originally from Colombia where I graduated as a Chemical Engineer from one of the country's best universities (Universidad Del Valle). I worked as a manager at a hydrogenation plant for a while. While there, I was able to collaborate with its construction as well as processes standardization. This early experience taught me a lot about the importance of standardization as the basis for long lasting improvement and workload reduction.

From there I came to the UK where I worked for different industries that specialize in spray drying, specialty chemicals, flavorings and emulsification, among others. After all those great experiences, I moved into the world of consulting which has given me the privilege of teaching my techniques and guiding different companies through their journey to what I call the Race (more about this concept later on). I have over 12 years of experience working in the trenches with incredibly good professionals; and during this time I have gotten to know more about human nature which, on its own, is the biggest cause of companies being left behind by their competitors, after all—at least in this day and age—organizations are not run by machines.

I used to think that the most important part of a company was its people, however I have learned through the years that a business has two critical assets:

1. Its best customers
2. Its best team members

Customers are not always right and there are definitely some you can do without. Employees who put themselves before the team and the mission tend to be a liability to the business. ***Companies themselves need to work actively to get the best customers and the best people available.*** When those foundations are correctly laid out, the secrets in this book can be applied a lot easier. *"The Flood, the Re-birth and the*

Race" is just a part of the puzzle, although a very important one.

I have purposely designed this book to be a light read, with no complex technical terms. (If you want some, I am an expert in ISO 9001 and 14001, HACCP, Six Sigma Black Belt, among others). I could have set this book to describe all that; however, something I have learned in my years of experience is that real sound reputation (I use reputation and Quality interchangeably) must be based on fundamental principles which international Quality Standards fail to explain. Such principles are what this book is about.

I call those principles secrets because they are real proven techniques that work. I have used every single one of them when leading companies through an accelerated journey where the speed is set by the management of the company, who decide how much gas they want to put in the improvement engine.

PREFACE

Do you feel like every time you go to work it is a lost battle? Do you shake at the thought of finding people so negative that trying something new is 10 times more difficult than it should be? Do you have so many daily problems in your company that there is no time to solve them all? Would you admit that each problem you "correct" comes back because nothing really has been done to fix it—apart from sending a random email asking people to pay more attention so it doesn't occur again?

Well, let me tell you, you are not alone. All companies have internal issues which are reflected by the amount of Quality complaints they receive. You see, companies are like the human body; the health of the different organs definitely reflects on the outside. The only difference is that a company is, arguably, a lot more complex in its processes. Bear in mind many of the systems of the body are automated (more on that later).

I encourage you to go to www.noelcardona.com/21secrets to join our community and access all the resources mentioned in this book.

If you are expecting a magic pill to get rid of the fat (bad reputation) your company is currently carrying around as it walks with difficulty, this is not the book for you. The methods described here require time, effort, discipline and patience as everything which is worth achieving does. As it happens in business so does it in life.

Even though this book has been written to appeal more to professionals working in

Quality; I am sure it can be used by any manager in any field, after all, as explained in these pages, everyone in any company should work at all times towards keeping and improving the reputation of the business which in turn will protect everyone's job.

SECRET 1. REMEMBER WHAT YOUR JOB IS

If I asked you what your job as a Manager is, what would you answer? Would you say your job is to fix ALL the problems in the business? If not, would you argue your job is to fix all the problems in your department?

If that is the way you have been thinking then I need you to stop right there, take a minute and breathe...because that is not your job. There are three concepts you need to understand to have clarity as to what your job really is.

The first one you need to understand is that there is no such thing as a "Quality Problem". There are Production Problems, Logistics Problems, Sales & Marketing Problems, etc. but no Quality Problems. The majority of issues in a company are generated by other departments. Sometimes the

Quality Department generates issues but as you and your team (if you have one) are constantly working on improvement, those issues are quickly and diligently fixed. On top of that, most of the time you are the one that sets the standard for how good the solution to a challenge is (unless you have a specific requirement from a customer or external standard). Sometimes it feels Quality is the police department of a business.

The second concept which is really critical is that to solve a challenge (that's what a problem really is) you normally need information from the area where it happened: how the different processes work together, the habits of the people working there, the methods used, etc. Nobody else in the company has a better knowledge of that area than those running it!

Therefore people must be able to fix their own challenges.

People that work in a specific area can easily give you solutions to certain challenges in that area. Sometimes it amazes me that people just won't take the time to implement already known solutions to their challenges but choose to suffer them forever while constantly complaining they don't have time to do more important work! (Sounds familiar?)

The third concept is to remember that time is limited. If you try to fix all issues yourself you will fail miserably: there are just too many challenges to be tackled in every company. Some of them are real, others made up, some important, others not. The thing here is that there are just too many alligators in the swamp for you to try to kill them all at once (*no animals were hurt during the writing of this book☺*).

Having said that, **your job is not to fix challenges; your job is to get others to come up with solutions and have the discipline to implement them. Along the way you must**

also make sure that the challenge has been overcome!

When you understand this, you can see that <u>*you are more of a coach than a manager;*</u> *and your job becomes more fun because you know you have to work with the whole company to create a new culture where everyone understands who they are working for and who pays their salary (Customers, not the owner, not the Managing Director, not the CFO. THE CUSTOMER).*

Now there is a point where some challenges become so complex that experienced employees, even your "experts" in the affected process, cannot fix them. Then, your job as a Manager is to use these cases as an example to teach your people when external resources should be summoned to assist in getting to a solution faster.

It is liberating for your people to suddenly realize they are not just operators of a process but managers of a system; it doesn't matter if they are machine operators or even senior managers. Think about this: a plant operative is considered a team member whose job it is to repeat a task many times a day, week or month with the least possible variation, and to report any issues as they appear. However, the best operatives are those who can see the system and present solutions to current and future problems. It is important to note that so called experts in a company are more of "Execution" experts, rather than "Fixing" experts and this is where they need your help.

As we will explore later on in this book, you will have to get your people to see the system instead of just the process. This means that your employees have the skills to zoom out and see the effect that their decisions and solutions are having on the whole company.

Your job therefore is that of a coach; one who can accelerate the journey of your people (the ones already working with you and future employees) and your company to that place where complaints are a rare occurrence. Of course even airlines which have the highest safety record in all industries have problems, however, if you have seen accident investigation documentaries, those issues are the result of incredibly especial conditions, and fortunately they are not the norm.

SECRET 2. START MEASURING IMMEDIATELY

Depending on the size of your company, and even if it is a small one, the measuring I am talking about here is at an industrial, heavy duty, dinosaur-sized level! Let's have a look at how a similar system would look:

I prefer technology-based systems over paper based ones. Why? Because applied properly, it makes a big difference in your long-term results. This switch has almost always resulted in the elimination of incredible amounts of waste especially when searching for information, which—if you stop to think—is something we are always doing.

At a particular company I did some consulting for, the system for logging challenges comprised of 5 different folders: Complaints from customers, Complaints sent to suppliers, a folder following actions from internal audits, another folder to follow up actions from external audits and a folder to log internal issues which also required addressing. The first sign of waste here is the multiple lists of things to do: the more lists you have the more difficult it is to plan, execute, and above all, to start measuring performance and cataloguing issues. Therefore you need a system which can integrate all those, so data processing can be done a lot easier as well as the follow up of each issue. Once you are doing that, you need to start extracting the numbers from your shiny new system.

A secret within this secret to set up a measuring system or as they are generally known, KPIs (Key Performance Indicators) is this: metrics should come out EFFORLESSLY from your to-do list. Ideally they should come out automatically so you and your managers do not waste time in the process of collecting data. Instead, the time should be used to analyze the current state of your reputation, and once you have started taking action, the effect of those improvements on the whole organization.

The way we replaced the 5 folders mentioned earlier was basically by using a project management system where each challenge reported would be logged. To do this, I recommend an electronic project management system which allows you to do the above and more. I normally use Smartsheet.com (I have no affiliation with them by the way). After many years of using it, the benefits are great. Obviously it is not the only system on the market and you may already have your own favorite; however, always remember that with the fast changing technology era we are in today, a new or improved system may come around. Always keep your eyes open.

To properly log each issue you will basically have to create a table where each column would contain information such as that outlined below:

a. **Each issue gets a unique number**: We used CAPA###, (i.e. CAPA223). This unique identifier is really important as you will need only this identifier to easily find any information related to this particular issue.

b. **Each issue is then catalogued**: Columns in the table were designated as: Short Description, Owner, Justified or Not, Date Open, Date Closed, Department, Classification and Source.

c. **Each Issue gets a Classification**: This is the same classification as in (b).

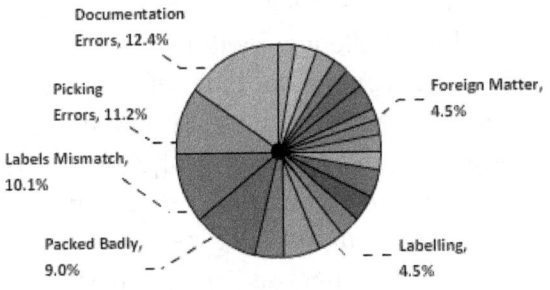

Figure 1. Categorization of issues is the first step to take
your company to the top.

But I wanted to highlight it because it is critical: Using as few categories as possible,
each challenge is given a category in order
to identify trends. In the context of this
book I define a trend as the appearance of a
repeat issue, either internally or externally.
For example, for a company where this system was implemented, a strong trend was
identified as Documentation Errors (see Figure 1). This trend then gave the basis to take
action in a certain area leading to stronger
processes as it normally should do.

The "As few as possible categories" advice is quite critical because if you catalogue two similar challenges within two different brackets you may not identify the trend on time. An example of this situation is a case which happened when analyzing data for a sales department: some issues were classified as "wrong product" sent to customers and some others as "Input errors" which were leading to the same problem. Once all

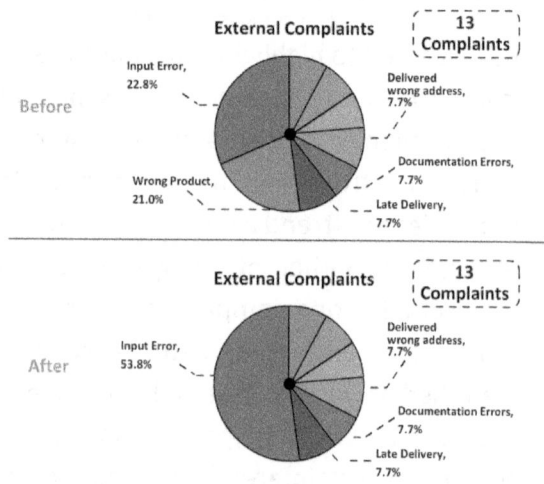

Figure 2. How trends can hide when too many categories are used.

the challenges received the "Input Error" tag the trend appeared clearly. See Figure 2.

d. **Each Challenge gets a "Source" classification:** Source tags I have used in the past are for example: Internal Issue, External Complaint, Supplier Issue, Internal Audit Finding, External Audit Finding and Risk. Those are the five folders mentioned earlier summarized with tags; very simple, very lean. If you need to see all the challenges of a specific category just use the filters these systems normally have and that's it: you will be looking at your electronic folder for that particular source category.

Once you have your issues categorised in a way similar to the one above, you can automate the system to tell you for example: How many external issues you have had in the past 12 months for the Sales Department, or how many internal issues originated in your warehouse. As you log and categorise each issue, the system will tell you (with little input from you) the information which is important enough to be followed up. This will in turn help you focus your time on analysing those numbers, and more importantly, to set prioritised actions (see the next secret) to create significant improvement in your business.

As a tool, *Smartsheet* has an extra paid application called Insights but there are also plenty of third-party systems (business dashboards)—which can connect not only to systems like Smartsheet but to all types of databases—that will allow you to extract and carry out all the calculations, to build graphs and any statistics you need, to know exactly where your customer's (Internal or external) pain is. I have used one of such third-party systems called *ClicData* extensively and so far it has all the features I need. Again, I have no afiliation with that system either.

SECRET 3. LEARN TO IGNORE

We, mere mortals, put our knowledge into boxes and many times we only use that knowledge within that box. What I mean is that as Managers we can analyze lots of data, filter out the main causes of a particular issue while "ignoring" the rest as noise. However when it comes to implementing or doing, either at a strategic level or on a day-to-day basis, many people are incapable of "ignoring" the noise so action can be taken on what is important, thereby falling into the trap of trying to fix everything at once.

If you already practice this secret you will probably have noticed that the majority of potential causes of an issue are, as I said above, only noise which does not have a significant impact on your challenge. Effectively use the Pareto Principle which says that 80% of your problems are due to

20% of the causes. If you work as a Manager you probably already practice this rule.

Now the secret here is not applying the mentioned principle to normal issues but to issues at a much higher level. As I explained before, in my years of experience I have always used electronic project management systems to log issues reported instead of pieces of paper, and as we have already explained, this single change gives you an edge over other companies.

I am not saying that the 80% is not important. I am saying that it can be ignored or postponed till after you have dealt with the 20% most important challenges. Here is something to remember: when you deal with the few some of the many will disappear. The reason for this is that some root causes act in synergy to create an amplified effect (cold air at high speed feels even colder for example), and some secondary causes are actually a side effect of the primary ones, the ones in that 20%. Another example would be if you were looking into increased fuel consumption in a truck, a primary cause could be the bad performance of the inner tubes leading to low pressure in the tires which is the secondary cause. If you resolve the former, the latter would disappear, at least not because of the inner tubes.

If you are in the Flood stage in your business reputation journey, you will have to learn to ignore the noise, focus and create positive inertia towards the change you want to cause.

You can actually ignore issues in two ways:

a. **Ignore the deep level:** As I mentioned earlier, your job is to make sure problems are fixed for good. When I say "ignore the deep level" I am talking about working mainly on the surface of the majority of your company's problems but allocating your time to root cause elimination for the one or two main issues affecting your business. This means you will allow your team to work only on corrective action where you know the challenge will come back again to find you (that is, you will have to apologize to your customer because, SOMEHOW, you got it wrong again). When you choose to do something, you choose not to do something else. The same applies here.

If you want to apply this technique you will need to keep logging the issues reported and make sure customers get what is needed to get this particular order right, but not look further until your main challenge is fixed. *You are not fixing the problems but you are showing your customer that you care about him/her.* This is easy because it is what people in different departments will naturally do. Their acts avoid the pain in the short term, ignoring the gains to be had. Ideally they should find and fix the source of the leak instead of just wiping the paddle over the floor. Working at the deep level takes a lot of energy, and unless pressed to do so, normal employees won't go there. However we will discuss techniques to turn those normal employees into super stars later on.

b. **Ignore in the Short Term:** Instant response from your part may be the source of all your problems. (Who would have thought?) If you are already familiar with *positive procrastination* then you know it means you must not jump immediately on each problem, stopping what you are doing. This is just a waste of time. If there are any critical issues which do require attention, you need to make time to find the root cause and fix them. You need to ensure you can focus and keep the main thing as the main thing until you can go to the next one.

How would you know which ones require attention and which ones you can solve at surface level? Well it will depend on the source of your challenge: I would say that if the issue is affecting your main customer you should put your resources there (20/80 also applies here).

The real secret here is to use the data you have logged to effectively find that 20% type of challenges and then focus with your team on those first, dedicating yourself to getting the people involved in proposing and implementing actions, and solving those issues for good.

For one of the companies I helped on their journey, after 6 to 12 months of logging and measuring, we found many issues but we noticed three main ones:

a. Late Orders
b. Picking Errors
c. Documentation Errors

Yes there were many more; but when we fixed those, the gain for the business reputation was huge.

Ignoring issues is actually a matter of prioritization, making sure other people take action at the surface while you start building the bases for long lasting systems which become a factory of solutions for customer happiness.

A very important skill as a Manager is that, upon receiving a report of a challenge, you should quickly evaluate the potential impact to the business reputation and learn to ignore it for the moment to tackle it in a planned manner.

"Ignoring issues is actually a matter of prioritization"

By now you will be asking, if I keep ignoring issues then this will have a big impact in the long term anyway, as there will be lots of unsolved challenges and consequently I will lose customers, so why bother? Well, let me remind you, if your organization is plagued with problems:

a) You don't have enough time to fix all the issues at once;

b) You may be losing customers anyway;

c) You need to start somewhere, and the best place is where the biggest impact can be created.

To find the light at the end of the tunnel, identify those big ticket items and then act on them.

There is a common journey for companies using this method: as big ticket items are solved for good, repeat issues disappear and then there is more time to work on challenges which in most cases are easier to solve. Your business will get to a point where your people will be spending a lot less time reacting to challenges and more time thinking about what could go wrong and fixing the system before it even happens. This is what is commonly known as being proactive or more technically, Risk Elimination. This is a very good place to be. Your company and every employee will go through a journey with three different stages:

"A company which works mainly on risk elimination is the best place to be"

---

1. **The Flood:** You have so many issues that you don't know where to begin, to stop leaks in your systems. There are so many alligators in the pond that it is difficult to keep your eye on the prize.

---

2. **The Re-Birth:** Having collected the necessary data, you get a handle on what is critical and needs to be tackled first and start allocating the most valuable resources (i.e., your best people, your time, also finance) to those critical problems. If this is done properly you will start getting traction and a culture of "yes we can" starts to appear where other managers in the company start seeing the improvement so negatively talked about as something that will make their life easier instead of more work to do.

3. **The Race:** This stage is where you have a full-on improvement culture with the majority of employees generating ideas, focusing on prevention and most importantly, knowing how to implement those ideas without destroying what already exists.

Note: For all stages of the journey it is important to always remember that destroying is ten times easier than building, and as they say, the road to hell is paved with good intentions. Good ideas badly implemented may be as bad, or even worse, than doing nothing.

At The Race stage the organization is a data-driven one in contrast to the first two stages where managing by guesswork is a constant.

"Every employee will grow as they take the journey through the Flood, The Re-birth and The Race"

To revisit the concept of 20/80 primary and secondary causes, as you and your company grow you will realize that as it happens in all other companies, especially at the first two stages, employees will complain that certain issues are due to lack of time; however that situation is only present because of a habit of only working at the surface (no work done at the deep level) when solving issues, leading to an accumulation of waste via the build-up of repeat issues.

As every employee goes through the same journey of growth as the company, your job as a coach for that growth becomes more critical every time, and oddly enough a coach needs to grow faster than the people he helps. What are you doing to grow daily?

I encourage you to go to www.noelcardona.com/21secrets and download two bonus tools I have created for you:

    a. **The Quality Journey Poster:** where I explain additional characteristics of these three stages.

    b. **The Tool - Questionnaire on your company stage:** a series of questions aimed at helping you understand where your company actually is on its journey.

SECRET 4. BE A MASTER AT TIME MANAGEMENT

It doesn't matter at what stage you are— The Flood, The Re-birth or The Race—you will always need three raw materials for improvement: Categorized challenges, Time, and Ideas for solutions. We talked about the first one in the previous secret and we will discuss the last one later on. For now let's focus on that intangible resource: Time.

Let's start with a calculation because I need you to understand, not just know, the real value of your time which you need to protect against two main enemies: the people around you and YOURSELF. Yes, nowadays we are our own enemies when it comes to using our time productively; more on that shortly.

Let's say you earn £60,000/year (which is not far off from a Salary in the UK). That would mean each hour of your time is worth

£30, assuming you work 40 hours a week. Now take into account current studies showing that in a whole day a Manager, due to interruptions, can only output 1 hour of productive work (yes it's that bad!). Factoring in this new information, you can see that each of your productive hours is actually worth £30/Working hour x (8 Working Hours/1 productive hour) = £240/Productive Hour. If you are a mathematician you can argue that the calculation should be done differently but we could agree to this differentiation: your working hours are NOT the same as your productive hours, and therefore you must safeguard your time as if it were water in a desert. Also, by knowing the real worth of your time, you should stop to think what tasks or projects you really need to be working on: always ask yourself if you should be dealing with an issue which can easily be solved by somebody else who would just sit down waiting for an answer. Would you pay an operative £240/hour to change the labels on a box? You may be doing just that without realizing so.

"Your productive hours are far more expensive than your hourly rate"

I mentioned before that there are two enemies when it comes to productive hours: The person who is always interrupting you, and yourself. If you have an open door policy that allows anybody at any time to come in and interrupt your work, then the generation of solutions and strategic planning, allocation of resources will never get done; if your office phone and personal phone are ringing one after the other you won't get anything done; if your email inbox is notifying you every minute with that annoying pop up window that you have a new message and you jump on to it each time, immediately switching tasks, then you will be at the mercy of others and never get anything done. I had countless days in the past that I allowed this to happen and it definitely had a drastic effect on my performance. When you are jumping onto tasks continuously, you are not being clever or efficient; the opposite is true. You get a lot more worn out than if you focused on tasks for a long enough period, partly because you are making mistakes by going so fast from one subject to the other. On top of it you get a little bonus, your people will get accustomed to your immediate response and expect instant action every time. This is a clear example of coaching your people, but in a negative way.

Think about what would happen if in an emergency room with just one doctor, every time a new patient comes in, that doctor leaves the one he is treating to see the new one: every single one would die.

Let me give you some of the secrets for getting 10X improvement in your work:

a. **Environment (Restrict Access to you):** Aim to create at least 3 hours daily of focused productive work (if you can create more, that is great). Disconnect the office phone, switch off your personal phone, do not open your inbox, and close your door. Also, identify any other common source of distraction for you and switch it off or block it. This will give you an incredible space where the big, critical and important projects are tackled and you are not working in function of others. Remember that environment is everything: if you want to become an athlete, get into a group of people with the same goal. If you want to take your company to the top, do what the top CEOs and Managers are doing.

"Actively create an environment free of distraction: from others and from yourself"

---

b. **Delayed Response:** Learn and train others to expect delayed responses. Probably by now you know that getting into the productivity flow takes at least 15 minutes and if you are interrupted every 4 minutes

---

"Email is toxic for productivity as it is your mobile"

(which is the actual average reported!) you won't even get close to that. Even though the development of email has actually enhanced communication, making it easier and faster, it has become toxic for productivity in the way many people use it: The get to work and the first thing they do is check their emails; responding immediately to requests of others, jumping on their agenda and forgetting theirs. This issue is such a distraction that even while replying the emails you already have in your inbox, you jump onto the one that just arrived, forgetting what you were just looking at. It is really toxic, so it must be controlled.

Here is some advice on practicing delayed response:

- If you have a receptionist or secretary, ask people to leave messages with them and you will return the calls, then block a day or two in the week to return all the calls. A mentor of mine blocks two days a month to return calls: How is that for a delayed response?

"Unlearning bad habits is as difficult as, or even more difficult than creating new ones! It is up to you."

There is a big wall here you need to go over to apply this: Yourself. I see you thinking: I receive lots of calls and I need to answer them immediately, I cannot do that! My advice here is for you to keep your mind open and answer the question of how it can be implemented. It is a critical decision to ensure you are not constantly working on other people's agenda.

- Only check your emails once or twice a week, when you are not in your peak productivity time. i.e., if you are a morning person like me, your peak productivity time is in that period. By doing this, you will notice that most of the issues, at the end of the day, have been solved by others. In an ideal world, eliminate emails completely: A mentor of mine refuses to use email because of how toxic it has become, and instead forces everyone to send faxes. He goes on to explain he does this because by doing so, people stop to organize their thoughts and requests instead of carelessly sending an email at the first idea they get. On top of that, the fax machine is at the office of his assistant who filters them, removing anything which is not important. In this way he only spends his time on the really important messages. If you don't want to go that far, a good idea here would be to get an assistant (it could be a virtual one) to review and catalogue all emails, only passing along what is important.

- Get people to book appointments with you as much as possible: By doing so, they will learn to come to you only with important issues and all the facts required. With time you can teach them that they have the capacity to solve most of their problems without your intervention. After all, what did we say your job is?
- Actively set response lead times for people: "Rob, I will work on your request but

due to my current workload I can only give you a response in 5 days" is a good phrase to keep in mind. Have you noticed that in the majority of requests you get there is no deadline? Well take advantage of that and set a date that works for you. Obviously the best deadline is when you can say NO: "Sorry Jane, I am afraid that is a request I can't help you with because..."

c. **Train your monkey brain:** It has been reported that 44% of our distractions on a normal work day are due to ourselves and nobody else. Almost half of the time our focus is lost due to our monkey brain wondering for no reason. Imagine that I have observed about myself that when I am in the "productivity flow" coming up with a new idea, I am remembering something that needs to be done every 5 minutes. I believe the amount of information and the multitude of distraction channels that exist today are leading people to a serious case of "Digiphrenia": attention disorder induced by digital technology, a term coined in the 70's. This disorder is causing people's attention span to get shorter every day, not being able to concentrate continuously for even 5 minutes!

This is why I recommend you turn off all devices. You would ask: but I need my mobile on in case something happens: if something is so urgent that it cannot wait 24 or even 3 hours, then you will not be able to avoid it anyway. That same mentor of mine who is extreme about time management does not

---

"It is up to you to decide how many interruptions you will accept, this is expressed in the way you design your environment and plan your week, month, year, etc."

---

have a mobile phone and uses only a communication channel to enable people to
contact him. Even his assistant works in a
different building and once a week she
sends him all the filtered mail, faxes and
messages, after which he plans and exe-
cutes responses in blocks.

A good tool to train your brain is to get a
stopwatch and challenge yourself to focus
for periods of 60 minutes and then have a
short rest. You will notice how difficult it is
for your mind to stay in one place for more
than 5 minutes. You are not alone. I seri-
ously think this is a new illness created by
the information age.

While reading this book, think about how
you can teach and multiply these secrets for
the rest of the people in your organization.
If you manage to have at least 3 full hours
of productive work per day instead of 1, you
would have increased the company's
productivity time by 10 hours a week. Now,
if you manage to do the same with 25% of

your people, the surge in productivity time would be amazing (250 hours/week if your company has 100 people). That is a lot of money in the works. A way I have seen this applied to a whole organization is booking all meetings in the company to fit into a single day of the week, leaving the rest free for execution.

If you feel uncomfortable reading these lines, great! Higher standards require more energy and people growth. None of those two are pain free!

Like everything else, it will always be up to whether or not you and your company have the discipline to apply these secrets. Many people will read this book but not implement a single thing; others will read it 3 or 4 times and get the most of it. Make the decision of which person you want to be. There are two things that no one in any industry has been able to put into boxes and sell: Discipline and Consistency. Most people require an external source of pressure to be disciplined. In this case, when building Quality and Reputation, you become that source, at least at the beginning.

SECRET 5. DO NOT PROVIDE THE ANSWERS

When a company is in the "Flood" stage there is something very common among employees: they are used to being told what to do and don't have the confidence to make decisions. This happens for two reasons: one, they are afraid of making mistakes and being blamed for it and secondly, their minds are conditioned to pass problems on but not to think about potential solutions, implementation and consequences of such actions.

You will find people who, consciously, do not want to grow and will not take any additional responsibility. There are others who want to grow but have not been stretched and trained to the point where they stop being just problem-communicators and become solution-providers. These are your hidden stars.

Average employees will only receive the training and education that the company provides, not looking to learn more outside the walls of their job. I say this because is critical that you understand that you need to become more of an educator than a Manager, more of a coach than a boss. As a coach, and make a note of this, you teach in two different ways: consciously and unconsciously. The former is when you are aware that, in some way, you are educating your people and the latter is when you lead by example. I would say the latter is a lot more powerful than the former. Actions erase words.

I have seen different cases where company directors will say again and again that they put Quality (reputation) first, but they will demonstrate with a single action (or many) that they don't really care. Basically, Quality in their company adjusts to the circumstances and not the other way around as it should be.

An example of this was a senior manager who decided to bypass the whole quality system because an issue represented £30,000. What is the price tag for you to put Quality second? That is a good question you should ask yourself and everybody else in your organization.

What is your price tag to bypass your Quality systems? £10, £10,000, £1,000,000...?

The management team or individual who consistently put a price tag to the preservation of their company's reputation (and that of their customers' businesses) are the ones who always ask why the company has so many problems!

Very timely for the writing of this book, I saw a documentary about how the Austrian wine industry went into a legal contract with Germany to provide sweet white wine. The Austrian weather in the year of the harvest was a disaster, leaving the growers with very bitter grapes. Not being able to meet up with the sweetness required, they were faced with two decisions:

a. They could pay the fine established in the contract as they could not provide the wine to the required specifications, OR (what do you think?)

b. Come up with a sweet wine and make lots of money!

They chose the second one. In order to make the white wine sweet, they hired a biochemist to come up with a solution. The biochemist, after a lot of research, decided to recommend anti-freezing liquid to sweeten the wine. The adulterated wine produced was sold to Germany. Initially they got away with the cheat scheme for two years, but when tests were implemented for the quality of the wine,

Germany realized the adulteration. The whole Austrian Industry was banned from providing wine to Germany; 2 million bottles were destroyed, leading to the total collapse of that Austrian business; not to mention that several people, biochemist included, went to jail.

So the question is, if you put a price tag on bypassing quality, how sure are you that the return on your investment will be a positive one? Almost always, that is not the case.

"The price you pay to bypass your Quality systems will always give you a negative return on investment"

The higher the rank of the person showing the wrong example, the more powerful the negative impact: "If the General Manager does it, then why am I being judged?" they will ask. In a nutshell, my point is that, by leading with the wrong example you are definitely providing a single answer for all quality challenges: do whatever you need to get it out of the door. If that is what you or your senior management are teaching, then surely you are in "The Flood" stage where the water is going up and the alligators are reproducing quite quickly. Companies like this require an urgent change of management.

> ## *"You Manage people when you give them the solutions, you Coach people when you ask them for solutions"*

Now, let's go back to the point of teaching consciously, which is the most powerful and the one I really want to point you to.

If your people bring a challenge to you and you always give them the answer, you are signing yourself up for a queue at your door. Such queue will be composed of paralyzed brains requiring the green light to go ahead with even the smallest challenge. It is very likely that if you happen to behave that way, then your superior also follows the same pattern.

If you really want to create a sound improvement culture, then you should stop providing answers to all the problems, at least to the ones people can figure out for themselves. You see, if you get into the habit of producing the answer automatically—which you will be able to do when experience has taught you the ins and outs of the job—people will expect a solution every time.

If you think deeply about this, there are two main issues here: First, you create followers not leaders; second, you have followers who, because they don't think about the solutions, will not collect all the information required to give an answer to the challenge. What this means is that you will have multiple interruptions with the same issue and sometimes you have to go and collect information yourself, duplicating some of the work your report already did. See how companies in the Flood stage actually waste time at the very moment?

By changing from "To solve that issue please do A and B" to "What would you do if you were the manager?" or "How would you solve this issue?" or "Please take an hour and come back with a couple of possible solutions"; you start changing people's mentalities, generating a whole different dynamic in the organization. Some people will resist at the beginning, they won't want to be blamed if the solution does not have the desired effect. However if you coach them through this process they will come out on the other side more confident of their own problem solving skills.

As usual the big obstacle in trying new things or building new habits is not actually your people, **it is you**. You will be tempted to just give the answer and not bother. Even after several years practicing this secret, the answers try to come out of my mouth automatically, but I have to stop myself so I don't create a follower. So this is not easy. You need to train yourself to hold the answer and coach your people through questions so they can arrive at the solution. This is one of the most important techniques to multiply yourself and create culture within the business. As we have said before, your people know the systems better than you do, therefore they are likely to find better answers than you could, after all there is more than one right answer when it comes to solving challenges.

As we will see next, in order to play this game you will need to teach your people the single most important rule required to skyrocket the reputation and quality of the products and services you provide.

SECRET 6. A GAME WITH ONE RULE

When a company says it puts Quality first, how does it do it in practice? There must be a way, because otherwise that statement is just a very vague phrase. Is it not Health and Safety first and then Quality Second? Well I can live with that ranking, but ideally Quality and Health & Safety should be up there together.

Think about this: every product or service complaint is an accident, one that causes a wound that does not heal. I say this because customers are easily lost after the accumulation of such injuries: your company becomes complacent when no additional complaints are received from a particular customer who, due to a repeat issue becomes accustomed to your bad reputation. However, when a new supplier enters your market they will offer the cure to these illnesses taking your customers away from you. Excellence is not easily re-placed, and excellence, as we will see later, has to do with attention to detail.

As I said before, this is a game with one rule; a very expensive game, in terms of your reputation as a business, and financially if not played correctly. Like everything else, you and your organization choose how to play it: you aim to get to first position or to be the last to arrive. The one rule is:

> *Quality has to be defined in a very simple, yet very precise way, so anyone making a decision to go with the product or service you provide, knows clearly what the way to go is.*

Your organization may already have one in place, and if it's working, it surely is something along the lines of the definition I have used for years:

*Quality is defined as conform-
ance to customer requirements on
the very first attempt, every time.*

That single rule has countless implications
which I would like to discuss further.

a. *Every single employee must ensure
    such requirements are written and un-
    derstood:* If customer requirements are
    only in people's brains, not properly
    written somewhere, somebody at
    some point will forget, and the **end re-
    sult** of that is **an unhappy customer.**

b. *Requirements come in two different
    shapes:* Tangible requirements and In-
    tangible ones. The Tangible ones are
    characteristics your customer explicitly
    indicates for every order such as deliv-
    ery date, amount, color, model etc.
    Intangible ones (not stated ones) are
    the ones that customers expect as "per

common sense": no scratches, uniform painting, lids properly tightened, no missing items in the order, etc.

A company dedicated to keeping or improving its reputation must have clarity about **ALL** customer requirements—both types—and make sure there are inspection points where those characteristics are evaluated. The key point here is that, if those requirements are floating in the air, there will be no way for them to be enforced. Obviously, tangible ones are easier to control but you must not forget the intangible ones. 25% of the complaints a company I once consulted for had, originated from a certain working

---

"If meeting customer requirements is dependent on employee's memory, you have a baldy positioned business"

---

process where operatives were letting 20 Liter containers go out of the door with loose lids, thereby causing leaks during transport, which also had a Health and Safety implication!

Having said that, how do you use this single rule to create leaders who are focused on improving customer happiness and company reputation at the same time? Easy (at least on paper):

a.   **Teach them the rule:** In the past, I have used examples similar to the ones presented above to explain how that rule can be applied to day-to-day operations.

b.   **Don't give them the answers:** As I explained before, 99% of problems can be solved at the level where they are created, therefore train your people—and yourself at the same time—to use that single rule to produce solutions in line with what you would do when an issue is reported. In other words, teach them the decision-making process you follow. This is a good way to multiply yourself.

Warning: remember that you will still be accountable for the decisions your people make, but train them to also understand this and ask additional questions when necessary.

c. **Teach them to defend the rule:** It is important for people in lower ranks to understand that they can, and should, challenge decisions of superiors which go against this rule. For example, if the Marketing Manager requests an assistant to make false claims on the advertisement of a new product, he must refuse. If the production manager gives an order to an operative to change the expiration date of a product for no reason, the operative must refuse. Not only do you need to train people in your organization to do this, but you also need to make them understand that when something similar happens, they immediately stop reporting to that person: there is a virtual switch in your company organigram where the person challenging a decision now reports to the Quality Manager. They need to be taught that they can do so safely with no fear of consequences. To prove this, just think about the fact that all decisions on what to do with products or services that don't meet requirements, are given to the Quality Manager!

"A virtual change occurs in all companies where people deviating from customer requirements, instantly switch to report to the Quality Manager"

What if the sinner is the boss of the Quality Manager? Well, apply the same rule; the Quality Manager in this case starts reporting to the next upper level above his boss.

If there is a group that needs to respect this rule, it is definitely the senior management level of the company, as they are the ones driving the need for a better image for the company, and leading by example. Therefore, they also need to be educated to understand that as soon as somebody is doing something wrong, on purpose or by ignorance; that person, if it is a manager, immediately loses authority over his/her reporter who can bypass him/her to bring the issue to a higher authority with no fear of retaliation. ***That is how an environment of transparency is created!*** Think of an extreme case where an employee, let's say a manager, is found poisoning some food or stealing from the accounts: this person now has to be reported to the police. The Quality Department is the policing authority within any organization!

SECRET 7. THE TRIANGLE OF QUALITY

It is important to understand that in order for you to be able to log and catalogue challenges coming from inside and outside of your company, people need to feel comfortable communicating those issues. However, this will not happen without an existing no-blame culture. No team member will report an issue if they feel they are going to be punished for it. Would you?

There is a direct connection between a culture that has people being afraid of taking blame and the "Flood" stage described earlier:

When you hide problems for any reason, they will just become bigger and multiply.

If all of your company's challenges are put in a room and ignored completely, at some point, the contents of the room will burst into your building, destroying everything on its way: A flood caused by a tsunami!

How then do you create such a blame-free environment? As usual, you need to start with yourself by understanding where all the problems come from. You really need to understand this concept (which is very different from knowing it) before you can actually teach it to other people.

From all my years of experience building and improving companies' reputation, I have learned that problems come from only four different sources; and of those four, there is one which is the most important of all.

First, let me introduce you to what I call the Quality Triangle. All your company's problems can be classified into four big categories:

Even though I only have approximate numbers, I can tell you that the different tiers are in the correct proportions.

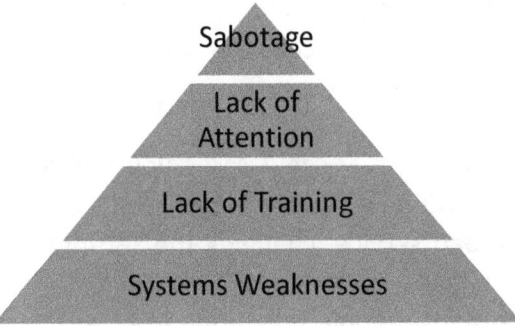

This triangle has wide implications in the way challenges are approached in every organization. Again, it doesn't matter what your business is, the REAL ROOT CAUSES of your issues can be classified into those four categories. What my experience and my mentors' experience tell me is that the percentage of issues coming from the categories above is more or less as follows:

a.   Sabotage: 0.1%
b.   Lack of attention: 0.4%

    c.   Lack of Training: 0.4%

    d.   Systems weaknesses: 99%

The proportions, as I said, may not be accurate to the decimal point; but certainly are in line with reality. Let's talk about each one of them:

Sabotage: In very few cases you will find people willfully damaging the product, giving a bad service, changing the settings of the machine, falsifying information, etc. The majority of people take pride in what they do. This is one of the only two cases that I agree and support that the person should be let go, as it is actually destroying the company from the inside, a little cancer if you will. This person is normally a very negative and unhappy one for one reason or another, and should not be allowed to stay.

Another case of sabotage, very common, is when senior management will put a price to Quality (as we have already discussed): If they see a case where money can be saved by hiding a problem, they will agree if the price tag is big enough. In that case, you, as a Quality Manager, can choose to leave the company or report to the maximum authority of the company, even to the owners if necessary.

Just for your benefit, the only other occasion where I would allow the root cause of the challenge to be connected to the person itself is when he or she is not fit for the job. For example, a job requiring a lot of concentration cannot have a person who is by default very distracted as he/she will become a danger to himself, others and the product/service provided. Hopefully proper recruitment processes will put the right people in the right roles.

Lack of Attention: We all make mistakes, we call it "human error" and we are more likely to make mistakes when we are tired. I make more mistakes in the afternoon than in the morning when I am fresh. I also make more mistakes when I fall into the trap of multitasking. My point is:

 Mistakes happen but people will not make them on purpose.

There is no single person I know, who enjoys redoing something up to two or three times, even if his/her job is repetitive. I am pretty sure you have had that feeling!

Lack of attention (human error) should not be an excuse for constant mistakes. If this is happening, then the methodology, work environment or even the person himself needs to be looked at in order to tackle this issue. Jack Welch of GE used to say that there are no issues with people making mistakes, the real problem is an organization not learning from them and making the same mistake twice.

A company in the Flood stage, and even one in the Re-birth one, will have the habit of accepting human error as the root cause of its issues. The less this happens, the more mature a company becomes in improving its reputation.

> ## *"The reputation of a company in the market is directly related to accepting human error as the root cause of its issues"*

As I really want to make my point here, think about this: when we talk about lack of attention we are basically saying the person forgot to do something. If your company is like the ones I have worked with, you are constantly giving your employees more to remember every day. If there is a weakness our brains have, it is that our memory is very limited! Therefore the combination of a bad memory and having more to remember is an explosive one, highly likely to lead to mistakes.

Lack of Training (Lack of Information): this is definitely one of the most important weaknesses of the companies I have consulted for.

Managers and supervisors are normally too busy to provide training to a level where people are proven competent. Most of that education is done on the job with no evaluation of learning goals—if there are any set to begin with. If we for a moment accept the blaming culture as something good, then the fault here would not be of the majority of the people working for the company but of those people who are in charge of making sure knowledge is transferred properly.

All employees need to understand that, in a way, any exchange of information is training, and when giving orders verbally for example, something as easy as: "could you please explain to me what I just said to check if you understood?" could be used as a test to prove communication has been successful.

There is something very interesting to note: the more manual systems a company has the more it relies on communication: verbal, written, graphic, etc. This means that the more we rely on people to remember to take certain action the more likely it is that at some point, no doubt, somebody is going to forget to do something critical to meet customer requirements.

A mature and successful company must identify what know-how is critical to meet customer requirements and devise ways to make sure that critical knowledge is always available during critical moments where it is needed (for example process procedures, checklists, etc.). It is not good to have a lot of knowledge stored in a way or place where people just can't or don't bother to access it. In the same way, successful organizations need to devise ways to transfer knowledge in a way it doesn't become cumbersome, and it is so standardized that everybody receives the same knowledge and competence can be validated easily; otherwise you will leave people to train themselves, ending up with different ways of doing things. When the road is not clear you may end up making your own.

"The less standardized and automated your training system is, the slower your customer will have competent people"

An example of what we have implemented in several companies I worked with is training people by creating videos of processes, and combining these with additional theories related to the process. As usual, a new technique will make people uncomfortable because they need to learn new skills (video editing for example); but it is worth it at the end of the day because you end up with a training tool which you can use over and over, and everyone gets the same knowledge. Besides it takes only a fraction of your time and you can use that fraction to evaluate competence. In effect, you are duplicating yourself via automation! Yes, people still need training on the job; but techniques like the one explained will give them a massive head start in the process.

In a mature company there should be a standardized training matrix for each role with ready-to-use tools for that training, as well as defined ways to check that the trainee is competent to carry out those tasks. After all, would you lend the company car to an employee with no driving license? Again, lack of training or information should only be accepted as the REAL ROOT CAUSE of a challenge in very few cases.

System weaknesses: This is the mother of all issues, at least in my opinion and experience. I would argue that the maturity of an organization is measured in terms of the resources allocated to develop skills. You can then use those abilities for each individual problem no matter how small, so it can drill through the different layers of the Quality Triangle and reach at the most important question you can ask during an investigation aimed at finding the root cause of a challenge:

Why did the system not stop the problem from happening in the first place?

To find the very cause of an issue there are several techniques available to use and one is the "5 Whys" technique where—you probably know this already—you ask "why" as many times as possible to get to the bottom of the issue. However, what we are not told when we first learn to use this technique, is where we should aim the analysis—in other words, when to stop asking "why".

If you understand the Quality Triangle, you will know where to aim your questions; which is right at the system level.

After many years of solving problems, I have been able to simplify my questions to the one above and thus look at the system immediately, why? Because people will forget, people won't get trained properly, at some point somebody will sabotage your process; and therefore you need the system to be your guardian.

I am not saying I have discovered the new gadget for management, not at all; in Japan the concept of "error proofing" was developed a long time ago. What I am saying is that I have gotten to understand this so well that I do it automatically. Again, as I have said before, it is not enough to know a concept; you need to apply it repeatedly to understand it.

Your job as a Manager is to teach people to work at the system level, aim to error-proof at all times so that there is a guardian stopping people from taking the wrong path and making decisions which can lead to mistakes.

"But WAIT A MINUTE!"—you would say—"in one of the secrets you said that we should create leaders and not followers, and to create leaders they need to learn to make their own decisions; now I am confused!" Well you are correct; it seems like a contradiction, but it is not:

You need to create leaders who can make decisions at a strategic level, aiming to meet customer requirements while at the same time implementing solutions which build company systems strong enough to stop mistakes caused by operators making the wrong decisions (choices) at the mechanical (repetitive) level.

I know that sounds like a mouthful, but it is pure gold! Let me explain with an example:

If a person has to enter a product description in a spreadsheet cell several times a week and the information is really long, that person may enter slight variations of it to save time (this is the wrong decision if you want to have a standardized record), if the system was strong enough you would add a dropdown list where the user only has to pick the description. Sorry for the simple example but I hope I made my point. In this example the owner of the spreadsheet should have thought at a strategic level to see that the system required standardization and propose the dropdown list as the improvement required to make it stronger. With this change implemented, the person does not have to decide what to write on the description but just choose from the list. A strong system guides the user and even controls his behavior. Yes, the person will still have to make a decision, but the window for error is a lot smaller, and on top of that the operator has to do less work: picking from the list as against writing a whole sentence.

Companies in the "Flood" stage have weak systems, where there is a lot of manual work. This manual work keeps your people busy at the mechanical level. When you reduce (hopefully eliminate) that type of work, your people can focus on the results and not on the process; thus getting the opportunity to think creatively and strategically. In turn they can see the big picture, aligning their actions to the company's global direction.

They say you cannot get different results by thinking in the same way you have done in the past. That is certainly the case here: if your company does not go past the human error level, your business reputation will not go anywhere, well at least not upwards.

I have to admit that to teach people to think deeply about system-oriented solutions is not easy at all, but that is the way if you want to achieve long-lasting change. If a solution depends on somebody remembering, you may be lucky if that person has a good memory. However, if that person leaves the company, the information will go as well, leaving you with no system.

A system is not necessarily a massive piece of the business. A system is a process with inputs and outputs, and can be as small as entering data in a spreadsheet as the example mentioned earlier. Take this into account so people do not use it as an excuse to not implement solutions because "it is too difficult". Remember that at the end of the day; a car is made out of nuts, bolts, plastic, metal and glass!

To make sure you understand this; when asking why something has happened, aim to test the system, push your people to find the causes at the system level, to redesign its working and turn it into a working tool for their day-to-day operation.

SECRET 8. GET PEOPLE TO DO MORE BY DOING LESS

I have learned over the years that a solution will only last if people feel it is helping them. The best solution, in line with what we have already said, is the one which both helps company and employee. It is the one that makes life easier for people.

I have worked on different projects throughout my career; in one of them, the time required to complete a job was one week and through breakthrough improvement I managed to reduce that time to two hours. Yes, that was the amount of manual work involved in that particular task.

Also, I have worked on projects where utterly complex processes have been reduced to mere operative input of the raw data with the system doing the rest.

It is difficult to convince an employee that he has to do more. However, it is a lot better to get that employee to produce a lot more while doing less work. Achieving such a result is certainly not easy at the beginning, but once the system is set up, you don't need to worry as much.

To do more by doing less, build systems which people can operate with less of their time and effort, yet give a lot more output. That output is measured as more accurate, higher yield, faster, cheaper, etc.

A good system is the one you can see as a tool: you know, almost from birth, that good tools instantly make your life easier.

"If a person is the system you instantly have a point of failure"

An example, I remember, was a project where someone had to do a very complicated production plan for one of the plants in the company. This exercise was so complicated that people used to call it SUDOKU; as they had to, by trial and error, allocate material until a certain target number was reached. The process was so cumbersome that it was causing an incredible amount of waste which was only noticed when the improvement was put in place. It took advanced math and lots of effort to simplify the whole thing. The operative went from 40 minutes required to create each plan to 5 minutes and she had to do circa 200 of those per year: that is about 116 hours or almost 15 working days in the year (8 hour working days) saved. If you have a good employee, those 15 days should be used for additional improvement, to accelerate your way towards entering the "Race" stage of your business!

As I mentioned earlier, doing this is not easy. Like everything, there are different levels of challenges but if you really want to make an impact in your business your people need to learn this essential skill:

They must understand a problem and devise solutions to strengthen the system so the root cause is eliminated, at the same time removing themselves as much as possible from it.

SECRET 9. TEACH THE HENRY FORD PRINCIPLE

A mentor of mine says:

"Focus on potential not on resources"

If you or your people are thinking about how to solve a challenge, and at the same time judging the likelihood of finding a solution in terms of the resources available, creativity will be killed.

Henry Ford said it better: If you think you can, you can. If you think you can't, you can't. Either way you are right!

In every company I have worked with I have found people preaching the famous phrase (which should have been put in a poster if it wasn't so toxic) "We have always done it this way, what you are trying to do won't work". As expressed by the Henry Ford phrase, thinking that way brings it to reality.

This practice usually seems to come from people who have been with the company for a long time and are settled in their ways, becoming negative to change.

Negativity can spread like a cancer to other people, especially the newest in the company who can be influenced easily if they see their negative colleagues as a source of experience and authority.

In my opinion, it is really dangerous to do something just because it works, without understanding why it does. If we took that practice and applied it to the whole company, the competitive edge would easily be lost. There would be nobody holding the knowhow required for improvement, which is basically an understanding of how things work; without it any company is helpless.

It is natural that people, especially employees, don't want to try new things and that we all are made technologically "obsolete" as we get closer to the end of our careers. However, improvement needs to be made; otherwise as competitors come up with new ideas your products will be made obsolete. Remember that obsolescence is not necessarily caused by time; but by new, more efficient or effective ways of doing things.

The point I want to make is that innovation starts at the very beginning where you tell yourself *"I know this is a complex challenge but certainly there must be at least one better solution than the one we currently have."* When you do this, as an act of magic, you start getting potential ideas for solutions from everywhere.

Need is the mother of all creativity; however, need comes from some sort of insecurity. Entrepreneurs are really good at developing ideas because they have the urge to create, and in many cases they run financial risk; therefore solutions must be found for every challenge. An employee, on the contrary, craves the security which a company provides. The longer a person works for a company the less creative he tends to be. I wouldn't say this is the only cause or reason but I would argue that it is, using our own language, a 20/80 root cause.

SECRET 10. CREATE INTERNAL ENTREPRENEURS

To create leaders and not followers you must teach them to behave and become the owners of their small business units.

In the same way many companies create centers of costs and engage each area leader so they can take care of their own budgets and not spend more than they should (a budget KPI); when working to improve the reputation of your business you should divide the business into high level processes, assigning owners to each so you can effectively drive accountability as we have explained before.

When each area leader can actually see (measure) the impact of their work within the organization they become more enthusiastic as their job becomes more meaningful: When they see the big picture they can actually complete any missing part of it, and that is what you want.

I call this secret "Internal entrepreneurs" because by creating small business owners you generate more than excellent supervisors, managers or leaders: you generate self-driven individuals who know their areas and how those areas are connected to others, who know themselves, know how to negotiate with their reports, can describe the most important numbers, and can solve problems in the proper way.

Your internal entrepreneurs, like any business owner, can direct or bring external resources to solve internal problems. I would advise you to teach yourself, and your people, to use sites like odesk.com or peopleperhour.com where you can hire freelancers for a short time. By doing so you can have access to professionals offering you specialized solutions, and work with your employees on projects; accelerating the speed of improvement, and in many cases, making it possible. However, your team will need you to set the path for them to follow. The freelancers can help with the details.

An important skill of entrepreneurs is persistence and consistency: to solve the big ticket challenges you need that. If your employees fail at the first instance and then give up, they are not really internal entrepreneurs. As a result, you may be getting the problem on your desk because they could not fix it.

To develop such skills in your people, you need to make them understand a very basic yet incredibly powerful fact:

The word "impossible" should never be written or said on its own. Instead, it should always be stated as "impossible with our current knowledge and technology".

Now, let's stop for a second and analyze that phrase so you understand it. First of all, when you just say something is impossible you instantly block your mind, you kill your creativity. Secondly, the phrase implies that you need more knowledge or different technology to overcome your challenge. Please note that you may not need new technology but a different one. You don't have to reinvent the wheel every time to solve an issue, what you need to do is to keep your eyes open for what others are doing in your industry, and even better, what others are doing in other industries so you can connect the dots. Always think about what was considered impossible a few years ago and now is simply part of our daily lives, which should be enough to help you:

Tackle your challenges with an open mind assuring yourself that the answer is already out here waiting for you to recognize it.

Produce your best so your people understand this and you will be a step closer to the "Race" phase of your journey.

Entrepreneurs have incredible and unique techniques to do very critical things, which normal employees should learn and practice:

They continuously analyze their performance and decisions to find ways to get <u>themselves</u> out of the way.

This reflects the fact that every person in the world is limited by his beliefs and techniques:

- *Beliefs dictate our own behavior*
- *Our behavior is the cumulative of our actions*
- *Our actions are leveraged through specific techniques to achieve certain results*

Therefore we are all limited by those two things: What we think and what we know.

A very vivid example is something I always teach the team of people I work with, and you can learn that in our next secret.

SECRET 11. THE MANAGER, THE FIRE FIGHTER AND THE OPERATOR

Teach your leaders, and yourself, to recognize these three modes or roles which to a great extent, we all chose to play.

On a daily basis there are many activities going on in a company, for example: a sudden issue that nobody expected but that needs to be fixed quickly, a piece of paperwork which needs to be handed to accounts as part of the normal work, a piece of equipment which requires maintenance, etc. Depending on which department you work in, *every activity can turn you into one of three different people* and therefore it is critical for you to be aware of them. Let me use an example that I like to give to illustrate this simply:

Let's say your job is to throw ping pong balls into a glass which is placed on a table and you have to aim and throw those balls one by one, meeting your customer requirement: balls inside the glass. As we all make mistakes, some balls will fall outside the glass, on the table, on the floor, etc.

Your employees could, unconsciously, have developed the habit of getting busy throwing the balls, aiming for the glass and picking up the balls which don't make it, to drop into it.

If no additional exercise goes into this process, you will have an endless activity more likely to worsen than improve. If you are not careful of this situation your competition will eat you alive.

Instead, your people need to learn to take time to *think into their results* and find ways to spend less time throwing the balls and picking them up when they don't make it in to the glass. This activity is critical. As you can see, every person in any company decides, on a daily basis, how much time they dedicate to throwing, picking the ball or thinking into how to eliminate those two from their schedule by strengthening their system and delegate whatever is not the 20/80 activity. Every employee at every level can do this.

Note: When the ball makes it to the glass that is an order meeting customer requirements, when it doesn't, it is a complaint. Picking the ball from the floor is complaint correction, thinking into results in improvement and risk prevention.

Taking this into account you need to ensure that:

All your people make time during the day, week and month—ideally at the beginning of that period—to think strategically as to what activities fall within:

    a. **Strategic / high level action** (Thinking into results)

b. **Repetitive / Operational** (Throwing the ball)
c. **Fire Fighting** (Picking up balls)

"Being self-aware every minute of whether you are performing the strategist, operator or fire fighter roles is critical"

With this in mind, your people and you can decide what to focus on, and as much as possible, delegate the rest to other people or machines or systems.

If you are in the "Flood" stage, many of your internal entrepreneurs will probably be working in the Fire Fighter and operator modes: Their agenda is dictated by the results of the actions of others which, given the stage you are at, we could say are actions leading to mistakes. This is a bad place to be because the solving of issues normally leads to more issues and it gets worse. Short term decisions are made in order to fix the problem at hand HOPING the challenge does not come back. In a way, an organization functioning on hope is destined to die, let's see an example:

A company with multiple invoicing errors chooses to bypass the existing system to correct the one at hand as it is quicker, breaking traceability to the original document trail. Then during an external audit of its accounts the organization cannot explain where certain expenses came from, in part due to errors made by an employee who that day had gone on holiday. As a result, a massive fine is imposed which just happens to be during a period of low sales, among other reasons due to an increase in "out of specification" products, resulting in loss of customers. The company goes bankrupt.

Does this seem like an extreme example? Maybe, but disasters seem to be the result of several unlikely events happening at the same time.

A company in the "Re-birth" stage is one where all its people start getting into the habit of stopping to think at a higher level, look at their numbers, prioritize and delegate lower priority or size challenges to lower ranks. In terms of what we learned in "Be a Master in Time Management", everyone, understanding the real value of their time and the impact it has on the mission of the company, therefore choose consciously what tasks they take on and which ones they delegate.

When you work on improvement—and everyone should work on improvement—there is a three-part recipe you need to follow and protect, which is time focused on using the skills that make you unique to solve the main problem affecting your company: Time, Skills, Main problem. Time on its own is useless. Skills without time are useless. Your main problem, without the time and correct skills given to it, can be very efficient at destroying your reputation.

When it comes to the "Race" stage, this practice is so engrained in the organization that the team actually requires additional resources to fuel the accelerated improvement activity which is happening.

It is for you, by tireless repetition, to engrain these practices in your people, to empower them and to give them freedom so they can develop their unit as the business owners they are, based on the rules you have taught them.

SECRET 12. TEACH THEM THE PERFORMANCE LEVEL REQUIRED

As I was writing this secret, now from Germany where I had to travel to do some consultancy, I had a discussion with someone who argued that getting to zero defects is impossible due to the cost to the company this exercise would incur. My answer to him, and to you, in case you are having the same doubt is this: As this is a game for which we have already set the most important rule, there needs to also be a clearly defined performance level required of your people, leaving no grey areas when making decisions relating to meeting your customer's requirements.

We have already discussed the fact that you need to define what Quality is in your organization, now you need to teach your team that terms such as "High Quality" or "Low Quality" DO NOT exist: there is just

Quality, if you define what the specific, exact requirement is, you are either in or out; and if you teach your people that you need to get it right the first time every time, you will be moving towards Zero defects very rapidly.

"A product or service is either in or out of specification. Therefore there is no room for high or low Quality"

There is a law in thermodynamics that says that all systems tend to move to a state where they use the lowest possible energy: you can see it expressed easily in how flow always chooses the easiest path to move through, how Iron prefers to stay in its oxidized state as it is more stable, etc. If you allow people to take the easiest route, i.e.

just send the product out on a gamble, hoping the customer doesn't notice, your reputation (Quality and company) are destined to die.

I always like to use the example of the companies which produce satellites: You can easily find documentaries on internet which show how they are made, and more importantly, the amount of tests that go into making sure the system will work as it is expected to. The reason for this, as you may have suspected, is that once up there nobody will be able to get to them to fix them: *it either works or works.* (I didn't mean "it either works or it doesn't").

I can see you, uncomfortable in your chair, saying to yourself: yeah right! But I don't make satellites, I don't need this. My answer to that is: as is evident in this book, the process to increase the performance standard in any company will start with raising the standard in the minds of the people who work for it. This exercise takes great effort to get new behaviors engrained, which can only be achieved by repetition. This is what I call an organizational habit: A group of people trained to behave in a similar manner while following set procedures. So I recommend you take a look at yourself. Are you up for the challenge?

While discussing with this person on the cost of zero defects, I explained something critical I have already said in this book: innovation does not have to be expensive, yet it can provide massive savings in your process. In my experience in innovation, the creativity used in adapting existing knowledge to a different use is the most important part.

Now, even if you never get to zero defects, your company would have moved towards a clear goal much faster with less input from you. One of my mentors says: "Money follows Clarity". Quality is all about clarity.

SECRET 13. CREATE ACCOUNTABILITY AT ALL LEVELS

We have already described the fact that you need to log and categorize all issues. This is the first step towards knowing your priorities. However it is only the first step. What you need to do with every single area in your company is to:

Translate the purpose of that area (high level process) into measurable indicators so accountability is created.

Let me explain with an example so you get the idea. Let's say you are working towards creating accountability in your Sales and Marketing Process. I would define this department's purpose as something along the lines of:

The accurate collection and communication, to other processes, of customer requirements to ensure the product or service is received on time and in full.

Let's analyze this purpose. The Sales department is the one which has the first and closest contact with customers and therefore needs to clearly determine what product is required, how much, which price is offered, what special requirements need to be fulfilled and by when. Once this information is collected it needs to be communicated to the production, warehouse or creative departments which are in charge of actually creating, assembling or designing whatever it is the customer wants. Also, this process needs to follow up other departments to ensure the order is delivered on time and if not, to let the customer know the situation.

Having established that, you can now define performance indicators for that Area such as:

a. External Complaints Originated in that process
b. Internal Complaints Originated in that area
c. Percentage of orders delivered on time
d. Customer Happiness
e. Delivery Speed

These are just examples of what I have used in the past, and the KPIs are different for each process. The important part is to make sure that the purpose of the area is described accurately with numbers. It also pays dividends when you define those KPIs, thinking about how easy it will be to collect the raw data. **Warning:** What I am describing here—depending on the size of your company—may seem straight forward, however it may take up to a year: you have to define the KPIs for each area and make sure that each indicator is described clearly, and calculated in a way that reflects what you need. You will find that a lot of fine-tuning goes into getting the whole system to work.

"If KPIs are not continuously used to generate improvement you are wasting your time."

Once you have the areas' KPIs defined, you can now start educating your people to think about problems in terms of numbers and break those numbers into trends to show the weaknesses of the areas (as shown in Figures 1 and 2 before). With the measurement system in place, you can then set performance goals for your people to achieve during a certain period. For example: If one of your departments is suffering from errors in invoicing, and its current state is 80% accuracy; you can choose to set a goal for the team to reach 85% in the next 2 months. If the goal is not met, then that team should be able to carry out an analysis as to why and propose corrective solutions.

Avoid setting too many KPIs as you can generate analysis paralysis. I would suggest a minimum of 1 and maximum of 3 per department. KPIs must generate action, otherwise they are useless.

SECRET 14. CREATE AN ORGANISATION THAT DOES NOT FORGET IN THE SHORT TERM

As I have mentioned before, an organization which remembers what needs to be done and makes time to get the important things done to solve its issues at the root cause level, is the one that ultimately will win.

The question is how you get all this done in an organization that has many internal and external issues and has everyone busy trying to put fires out. Well, the answer is easy and difficult at the same time.

Easy Answer: You or your Quality Manager need to make sure that every area leader makes time to present solutions to the open issues which need to be solved. However, this "makes time" needs to happen at a constant rhythm to ensure the organization's

Quality heart beats as fast as possible. In plain English, follow up meetings every one or two weeks with a well-defined agenda and time limits.

"Difficult" Answer: The creation of such agenda should be derived from a master list which holds all the issues which are logged in the system but readily available and filtered for each area so there is no time wasted in the preparation of such meetings.

> ## *"The Quality heartbeat of a company at the Flood stage is very slow, sometimes close to a heart attack."*

I have implemented this dynamic at different companies by creating a "Score Card" per area which looks like Figure 3.

A score card is formed by three important sections:

a. The KPIs for a particular area
b. A summary of the recent issues which have occurred in that area
c. All the open actions and owners who need to attend the meeting.

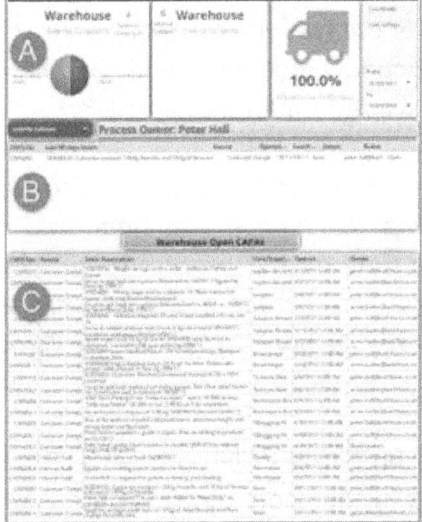

Figure 3.Example of a process Score Card

This score card becomes the heart of your improvement system, driving accountability with no time wasted to create it every time you schedule a meeting. I know you can see the document in detail in Figure 3 so I encourage you to Visit www.noelcardona.com/21secrets to download a full page example of this.

Whatever the way you do it, make sure that your functional meeting agenda and KPI reports are as automated as possible:

Your people must focus on making decisions with the numbers at hand and not wasting time on the process to get those numbers. This is where the organization accelerates its pace to get to the "Race" stage.

The reason I have called this secret "to remember in the short term" is because the score card makes sure that tasks, which otherwise would be forgotten, are tackled as quickly as possible, leading to the solution of problems from the root cause. Forgetting the actions proposed to overcome challenges will basically lead to repeat issues or slow response to your customers. This is where your company's attention to detail starts to make a difference.

SECRET 15. CREATE AN ORGANISATION THAT DOES NOT FORGET IN THE LONG TERM

We have seen how remembering in the short term is important and how to do it. Now let's talk about doing it in the long term.

My apologies in advance for the crude example: you can put a nail into the wall with a hammer, a shoe, a stone or any other thing, the critical piece of the puzzle is the knowhow to put the nail on the wall. The same happens with your organization: if your company as a whole loses its know-how, you will lose the most critical part of your operations. The equipment will remain but you will not know how to use them or use them optimally. I have worked with companies which—due to the patterns of certain processes, people leaving or managers making improper changes—destroy their current systems and consequently forget how to make their products or provide their services! Not a good position to be in.

There are several ingredients to brew the cure to this issue but I would like to focus on one here:

If the knowhow is only in people's brains and they leave, they will take that knowledge with them. Therefore you must understand that you are in a constant race to retrieve that information from your team members and share it with the rest of the organization.

There are different ways to collect as much knowledge as possible, but the most widely used is to: Get your people to write down what exactly they do. In other words, create procedures. Now there is another way which is even more powerful but not as widely used: Recording videos of your people explaining how they do their jobs. There are two massive gains from these:

First massive gain: A video will give a lot more details than a written SOP in a shorter time.

Second massive gain: A video is a much better training tool for your people than a written document.

Now, I know for a fact that in many cases you need written SOPs to keep records of your processes; in cases like that you can use both.

Obviously there is a downside; you need to learn a new system to create, edit and update the videos when required but I truly believe it is worth it.

Tools such as video cameras, video editing software, computer screen recorders like Camtasia are easily available via the web to get you started with this new way of doing things. You will also have to get your people used to being recorded: you will find some shy ones and some others who may win the next Academy Award!

Whatever way you choose to retrieve the knowledge, you need to identify the critical areas that you will start with; and I would advise that those closer to the manufacturing of the product or providing of the service should be the first ones, as that knowledge is one of the most important pieces of the puzzle.

Knowledge is never static: The organization will generate new ways of doing things; forgetting about the less efficient ones, new technology will come into your systems, etc. The updated knowledge should continuously be included in the systems you have created.

The best piece of advice I can give you in this secret is to have somebody in charge of knowledge management. A simple way is to have a system of documentation control with one or two people named as Documentation Controllers. (Bear in mind that documentation is any piece of recorded knowledge which is critical for your operations) And this is the key part:

Any changes to the knowledge should be evaluated and authorized by your documentation controller so no damage is made to the current expertise, making sure the obsolete one is removed.

A centralized point where changes to the current knowledge pool are methodologically introduced is critically important for your operations. It is important not only to make sure your documentation is preserved, but also to ensure the modifications which can severely affect your knowhow in a negative way are evaluated and analyzed properly before approval. This single step will prevent a particular weakness in companies working in the Flood and Re-Birth stages: **Jumping to implement changes with no evaluation of the negative effects it may bring.** This is like jumping from a cliff without looking at the bottom.

I always remind people of this fact: good knowledge systems should outlast employees so your company does not suffer significantly when team members leave the organization. I say this because capturing all the experience a person has is almost impossible in practice; at least in this day and age (maybe in the future we will be able to do it). In summary, my point here is:

Knowledge management systems are basically communication systems and the core use of systems is to store knowledge to serve as guides for the operatives who run them.

So always ask yourself and your people: how are you capturing your knowledge so you are able to communicate it to the people who will be working for the company in

10 years' time? In other words, people who haven't even started working for your business. If you can answer properly then you are in a good position.

> ## *"A tank is to water what a system is to knowledge: the function of a system is to store knowledge"*

It is difficult to say this but I need to include it here: the ideal system is the one that can replace the human input completely, leaving no room for error. However, taking a process to that level takes a massive amount of work. I am saying it is difficult, not impossible.

Just remember that if we introduce new knowledge and do not remove the one we are not supposed to use anymore, it is likely we will have different people using different methods; and therefore different outputs will be obtained thus increasing the variability in your operations. If the change in methods somehow impacts Health & Safety in your company, this approach is even more critical.

SECRET 16. TEACH YOUR ORGANISATION ABOUT EXPERIMENTS

Any change to your systems must be understood as what it is: an experiment which intends to reach an output in a different way, aiming to at least maintain or improve the one which was being produced before the modification was introduced. In plain English, if you change it and make it worse you have failed.

For example, if you have a car and you decide to change the engine, let's say you do this for two possible reasons: you want to be able to drive faster or drive easier, but at least at the same speed as before. In the former you want to increase the output level, in the latter you want to maintain the output but do to it with less effort.

There are two basic things to understand when it comes to changes:

a. If the output is affected negatively (if your car goes slower), the effort and money used to implement such change would have been wasted.

b. If the output is maintained but it is a lot more difficult to arrive at, then the change won't be sustainable because it will cost more effort and money. Remember people are more likely to take on changes if those make their life easier.

Now, if we define the success of a change in terms of a pre-planned output level then the only way to know it has worked is to measure that output before and after the change (Do you feel like we are always going in circles around the same basic principles?).

If you are familiar with improvement principles then you will remember that the state before the change is called the "baseline".

Measuring that original state in a defined and consistent way is critical before you even consider any actions to overcome the change. Why? Because in many organizations—especially the ones at the Flood stage—people "feel" or "believe" they have certain problems; however when you measure the baseline to start tackling that "issue", you find out the problem actually does not exist and it is only part of what is called the natural variation of the output.

Let's illustrate this with an example. Operatives of a plant "believed" that a certain product had too much dust (output) and changes would have to be made to reduce the amount of that dust; however, when a way to measure the output was devised and used, it was found that the levels of dust were within industry standards. No action was required. So as you can see from this, in the Flood stage you are not only sinking in real problems but in others which don't exist in the first place.

In order to move to new stages, your people should learn to measure that baseline, bring you the data and a potential solution which includes a way of measuring the new state of the system.

It is important also to understand that any system you are working on is a subsystem, a part of something bigger, and therefore any changes applied to a part will affect the whole.

Using the example of the car engine, the change will affect the total weight of the machine, the fuel consumption, the tire's service life, the steering wheel, etc.

This being the case, you must teach your organization to carry out a proper analysis before the change is initiated, in terms of what needs to be done to mitigate the negative effects. With every successful change comes new knowledge which has to be incorporated into your organization's brain and therefore the whole knowledge protection system we discussed before goes into motion. A good technique which is used in the design of systems is the one called HAZOP (Hazard and Operability Study). This method gets the user to set up different failure scenarios, prompting thinking into modifying the system to prevent a negative effect during implementation. Similar techniques should be used to imagine, or better, simulate the system before is created so major pitfalls can be fixed.

SECRET 17. INTERNAL MARKETING: RAISE YOUR PROFILE TO GAIN AUTHORITY

Do you see a connection here? In one of the secrets we were discussing how you need to create internal entrepreneurs and now we are saying you need to do internal marketing. What I found over the years, and maybe one of the things I enjoy more about working in improvement, is that you become a business owner within the business:

a. You need to coach all areas to make sure every process is working as it should, and also that the teams in each area are implementing the agreed improvements.

b. You need to find and bring special resources when the challenge is bigger than the organization's capacity to solve them.

c. To break barriers and get people work-
    ing together between areas in which
    communication is not effective.

d. To ensure that people who are NOT giv-
    ing you the necessary results on
    purpose are passed onto higher levels
    of the company for their behavior to be
    corrected.

e. You need to continuously educate peo-
    ple to remind them of the objective:
    customer happiness. Also, of the rules
    and secrets we have discussed in this
    book; effectively the basic rules of a
    well-played game.

I could continue but you get the idea.

Internal marketing should be heavily loaded
with what in the industry is called "Lessons
Learned". I would define internal marketing
as:

The internal advertisement of rules of quality which need to be present in people's minds, illustrated via examples of lessons learned during successful and not so successful projects.

In other words, use all possible opportunities to bring examples of what the team has achieved (or not) and how it is connected to, for example, customer requirements, proper change implementation, system weakness derived errors, etc. As we have said before in this book, your job is to create a culture and such a culture can only be formed in people's minds by constant repetition and linkage to fundamental rules which protect the reputation of your company.

As I have said before, the best way to bring negative people on board is to show them that something that they originally said would not work, is not only successful but makes their life easier. This kind of gain can open doors which would be impossible to open just by using words and motivational speeches. Remember, influencing people is easier when you lead by example and not just by theory.

With such an advertisement you will be able to achieve two things:

    a. You will create the culture that we have been discussing.
    b. You will publicize results of your work to the whole organization.

The latter will give you authority over your people who will see you as knowledgeable, capable of tackling challenges, and someone they should listen to when you bring projects to them. Also, if done properly, you position yourself as someone who makes their life easier and should therefore be involved in issues or anything that could potentially affect customers or their processes. Not to mention it will be noticed by the senior management of your company, who will acknowledge the value you are bringing to the organization.

Your internal marketing can be done via email, notice boards, conferences, meetings, training sessions, etc. Anywhere you can create the opportunity to go through this exercise is great.

Always let your internal marketing show the important work that other team members are doing; do not make it about you, if you choose to follow that route the final result will be the opposite of what you are trying to achieve. Done correctly you will make other people shine and you will as well. This is effectively an exercise of creating culture by positive reinforcement.

As in normal marketing, customers are gained by repetition and follow-up and for that you need discipline.

SECRET 18. REWARD YOUR PEOPLE WHEN THE GOAL IS ACHIEVED

I have always said that goals have two purposes:

    a. To know when you need to keep pushing: you can clearly see you have not achieved it yet.

    b. To know when to stop and celebrate.

All these processes, if done mechanically and regimented without taking into account human nature, can become monotonous and boring because teams reach the goal set but there is no celebration of any type.

Organizations in the "Race" stage have an advantage over those in the "Flood" and some in the "Re-birth" that know when they have arrived at the gate.

If your company is not a data driven one, two critical things happen: first, there are no clear goals as you are not measuring your position; second, you normally don't know when you have arrived. Given those two conditions, it is difficult to reward the team's achievements.

The exercise of clearly defining your goals in a measurable way requires you and your team to think clearly what the problem is and understand it before you can actually define how to measure it.

An example would be a case where you be-lieve you have an issue with a product which normally is brownish but this time has come out of the process white, as it happened at a company I was consulting for. To attempt to solve this problem you should ask ques-tions such as: Is the color actually important? Is it a customer requirement (stated/non-stated)? If it is important, how are you going to measure the color? What is the normal range? etc.

Connecting what we have learned here with other secrets in the book, once you have set the priority challenges which the organization needs to focus on, you can then set a reward for the organization when a measurable target is achieved.

As I have described before, if you have a system of performance indicators which cascade down to different individual areas, you can choose whether to link the reward for the whole organization to the top global KPIs; or to link special recognition to individual teams for particular projects which have a big impact in the global performance of the company but need to be tackled from a particular area.

Really great companies get one of those KPIs and make it a theme for the whole business to be aligned to; and depending on how long it takes them to achieve that goal, they will set a different theme every quarter or every six months.

Whatever way you choose to do it, make it visual, so a sense of achievement and competition is created which greatly helps your efforts to arrive at the goal even faster.

SECRET 19: BE PATIENT, IT TAKES TIME

The successful application of these secrets is not a quick fix, but should not take more than a one to three year period before you start seeing some important results. (I can certainly help you accelerate that journey. You can contact me on info@noelcardona.com).

As we know, people are creations of habit and organizations therefore are the result of the combination of the habits of each team member. It is sort of a collective brain. If the habits of the people are habits of low standards then that would be the general outcome. This is why to improve the reputation of your company, the change has to come from the inside—from a change of mindset of the majority of your people—else good PR is a short-lived and poor solution.

The secrets we have presented in this book may not really be secrets to some readers, whereas for others they are real revelations. Whatever the case, there is something very true which I have found in every one of my endeavors:

The number one reason for failure is lack of consistency

This means that the majority of people and organizations do not have the discipline to finish what they started. This can be attributed to:

The number one reason for lack of consistency is distraction.

Due to the overload of information, opportunities and market pressure we currently have, many companies cannot sustain their focus long enough to finish the projects they started. They are severely affected by the *"next shiny object syndrome"*. If this is the case for your business, then what you started was either not actually needed, not planned properly or the market changed radically, stopping the need for what you were working on. I would say the latter is the only justifiable one.

The successful implementation of these secrets is going to be based on two simple yet powerful factors:

a. **Clarity:** your organization must have absolute clarity of the goals that need to be achieved. This needs to happen at both strategic and operational levels. In other words, all the sub-teams must be aligned toward a clear path and a clear arrival gate. Also, each member of each sub-team is aligned to at least the objective of moving his/her area ahead which in turn moves the company forward towards the same overarching gatepost.

b. **Consistency:** Your team needs to have a meeting regime where the status of such goals are reviewed, corrective actions are set and ideally auto analysis of each area is done to determine where those obstacles are: sometimes they are financial, others may be from the growth of the business, many times it has to do with the skill of your leaders to break through obstacles (That is where internal masterminds are useful, see next secret). I would recommend operational meetings about every fortnight and then a global one every month, to review the status at a mid-level every month.

Also, strategic sessions where senior management evaluates the information gathered in the first two meetings and reviews the strategic goals set for the business.

SECRET 20: INTERNAL MASTERMIND

You are probably familiar with the fact that successful business owners actively participate in such sessions and you should have something similar in your organization.

The mastermind technique has been known for years and it is a process by which participants greatly accelerate their progress towards their goals by bypassing a lot of the learning that, by trial and error, the rest of members of the group had to go through when dealing with similar challenges in the past. They learn from one another's mistakes.

Masterminding is an effective environment for thinking and self-analysis where everyone is a coach to everyone else and the knowledge of different industries comes to-gether for the application of already existing knowledge to new fields.

In the case of your organization, your em-ployees would benefit, initially by getting feedback from their colleagues in an envi-ronment where no blame or fear exists and where the improvement of the individual is first.

Masterminds need to be organized effort:

    a.   No negativity should be allowed and all feedback should be constructive.

    b.   Members should be chosen care-fully. Hopefully they would be the key champions you want to grow.

    c.   There must be a coordinator who guides the sessions and who has the final say of whom can or can't be-long to the group and who needs to leave the group. This is due to the fact that a masterminding is a very delicate environment and therefore ultimate care needs to be taken no to break it.

d. It drives action, specially oriented to improve the person and focus on high level issues to ensure break through progress is achieved.

In external masterminds, you would normally aim to include high achievers with a "can-do" attitude. Members who aim continually to improve themselves, resulting in ever growing powerful leaders.

Imagine something like that for your organization where your team members can look at themselves and notice that, in most of the cases, they are the obstacles to get to where they need. To allocate and drive resources, to innovate, etc. That for me, is priceless.

I would suggest you start by identifying the stars in your business and bringing them to start that journey. Then through internal marketing you keep identifying and bring others to the group. From experience, people open up during these sessions and can connect their personal goals to those of the organization creating a much more meaningful work to go to every day.

SECRET 21: DEVELOP YOURSELF, DON'T BECOME OBSOLETE

We all either become obsolete or more valuable. We either keep learning or keep repeating. We either sink or float to the surface. It is your choice.

As you have seen throughout this book, there is a skill which is vital for you and your people to get, to drive improvement:

Improvement is only possible if sound solutions are well implemented in a process.

Solutions to problems come either from experience where similar challenges have been solved in the past; or from innovation, either on a small or large scale, where knowledge is applied in a different way.

Solutions are effectively the output of information from your brain, and this information must take into account the different parameters, constraints and desired outcome to be effective.

The key point here is that solutions will only be produced by your brain from the information it holds. Therefore it needs to have a constant input stream of knowledge, hopefully from different fields or industries for the solutions to be creative.

You need to make sure that you and your people are continuously learning about different fields in order to increase your "solution reserves". It is important that knowledge comes from different industries including yours, as you never know from which angle a challenge is going to come: sometimes issues are equipment related, some others people related, safety, hygiene, IT, etc.

It is also important to remember that your job is not to solve problems but to get other people developed so they can do so.

As technology develops, waste is removed from processes, accuracy is increased, stability of machines improved, errors removed, and in general, points of failure of your established systems become easily removable if you keep ahead with technology.

A way to keep ahead is our newsletter **"Business Excellence"** which has been created especially for you and your people to easily keep up to date with development in technology and other fields that can help you remove weaknesses within your systems. To subscribe please go to *www.Noelcardona.com/newsletter*.

Somebody said that innovation begins with imitation. That is very true and you should look first at your own industry for solutions which are already working. However, keep an eye on solutions coming your way from other areas; and keep your mind open.

BONUS SECRET 1: APPLY IT TO YOUR LIFE

Yes, I know you were only expecting 21 secrets. As these are extras, you can decide to skip them. (I would not do so. ☺).

As you need to become a leader and teach your people to define problems, measure and solve them properly, I would advise you to apply to your life as many secrets presented here as you can. The reason for this is that: by doing so, you will learn things you will not ordinarily get from theory. For example, as I have my own personal KPIs, I have learned that KPIs work better when the goals you set are close to the current baseline—that way there will be an effect of "being close" to the goal (clarity)—and therefore arriving at the final gate becomes a stream of celebrations, instead of just one celebration!

I did this when I set for myself the goal of running 300 km in a year (I know it is not a lot but doing it was an achievement for me). What I did then was to set small goals of 25 km weekly or 5 km daily. When I know I have to run 5 km at 6 pm on Monday, the action I have to take is very clear with no ambiguity; there is no escape. The way the human brain works, it feels more compelled to think about 5 km than 25km.

In the same way you will learn other important things such as the fact that once you define and start measuring a KPI, you have to stick to it to optimize the gathering of the data and see what flaws in the system may actually affect that number. The definition of a KPI may have certain flaws and therefore the whole process needs to be validated to ensure consistency.

By setting goals for yourself in the way you would for your company, you learn with time to easily describe problems numerically; so that you can quickly point out the measurable characteristics of a problem and define the expected output.

You also learn the virtues of being a professional time manager, the advantages of keeping up with technology, the difficulties and rewards of teaching people to come up with solutions themselves, etc.

When you join a mastermind, you will notice the incredible growth that you have gained; as you will become more aware of your limitations, beliefs, behaviors, and get feedback from other professionals in your area.

It is important for you to practice each secret and interiorize it. I have said many times before that there is a very big gap between knowing and understanding. For example, for you to generate solutions that point directly to system weaknesses—ruling out other causes which only point to the human input level—you must have understood the Quality Triangle (which is so

simple, yet so powerful to influence the reputation of your business).

BONUS SECRET 2: MAKE IT A GAME!

Training people successfully requires taking certain elements into account:

a. Concepts explained in a manner simple enough for the audience to understand easily.

b. Gradual increase in the complexity of the concepts (difficulty) as the training progresses.

c. Multiple repetitions of the same concepts in a short time for the trainee to get familiar with them faster.

d. An environment that allows the trainee to "fail" and learn at the same time.

e. A way of making the process fun to help the audience keep their attention focused on it.

f. Evaluation of the concepts learned to ensure the trainees have captured at least 60% of the most important knowledge you have transferred.

There could be more, but I will stop there. If you observed from the break-down above, a game designed for learning has all those characteristics. What we are talking about here is the "gamification" of your training.

*A **very good test of somebody's mas-tery of a concept is their ability to make a game out of it.***

I have been using this secret for some years now, and it definitely increases your people's engagement with what-ever training you are doing. It takes more time to prepare a session when you have to design a game, but it is def-initely a lot more powerful.

I encourage you to think about how you can make a game out of your training to suit sales assistants, operatives your executives, etc. For example, in the past I have designed games for hygiene where it is important for operatives to understand why it is necessary to do certain checks; to understand the basics of risk management; warehouse goods-in games to get people to play around with the different rules for different types of materials which would normally be received, etc.

If you noticed, in another part of the book I explained a ping pong game used to illustrate the concept of processes operator, manager and fire fighter.

Consider adapting the scheme of, for example, board games to your needs: for example, if you use the structure of Monopoly as base to design a training on building security it is much easier to get a working tool which you can use again and again.

Gaming is being used extensively in many different industries and the truth is, it is not that difficult to create one. You will need to have clarity of the concept you want to explain, and a system to award points. You can include buzzers to compete, with questions and answers, a simple prize for the winner, question cards, etc. I encourage you to join our community to get more ideas which can be implemented to facilitate knowledge transference within your team. www.noelcardona.com/21secrets